Companies Hire Employees and Then What?

Plan, Organize & Prepare (POP)

CHARLES DEVENNEY

Dedication

This book is dedicated to the Leaders and Influencers in my life:

POP – nickname for my Dad: Pat Devenney, the greatest inspiration a son can have.

Sanny White – a football (soccer) legend in Paisley, Scotland for his passion, devotion and drive to make the Craigielea Star a wonderful team to play for; and an appreciation for believing in me as a player and a person.

Jan – my wife without whom nothing is possible – my motivation and Guardian Angel.

Our exceptional off-spring: Bryan and Sarah and their supportive spouses Laura and Adam respectively and their wonderful children: Cormack, Corbin, Conlan, Paisley and Lochlan – the best kids in the world and who make our life revolve!

Thank you

About the D2SM Web Site

This website has been designed by my supportive collaborator: Laina Groom.

www.d2smbusinesssimple.com

To see the wonderful technical experience that she brings to life; visit the website, and enjoy the interaction and explore what fresh minds can do for your business.

Our belief is in simplicity of action and contact:

'SEIZE IT BOLDLY and DON'T DO IT SMALL'

Quote attributed to Berkshire Hathaway VP, Charlie Munger's 'grandfather'.

I believe wholeheartedly in the power of employee's being recognized as the best resources that a business can possess.

By working collectively, each company can benefit from having many minds focused on the BOSS! Otherwise, known as the Customer! We must seize every opportunity to interact with the 'Boss' and enter into a long lasting relationship built on trust, connection and belief.

We hope you enjoy the book and the website – as ever we will continue to add content and emphasis on our beliefs and passion.

Objective:

Inspire 1 Million companies and employees to integrate Customer Experience and Operational Excellence in their Business Practices.

Refers to UN Sustainable Goals #17 – Partnerships

Valuable Contents First

Part 1   HR Due Diligence   1

Underneath this heading is a collection of activities that most companies and corporations try their very best to achieve. Few succeed! The reasons for failure are numerous and are the basis for more commentary by me later. By gathering the material as observed and assembling them inside this book I have chosen to do it in a manner that is brief, concise and factual. Many stories surrounding my time on the shop floor and corporate offices are available and will in time be released for an audience that will be composed of very serious readers of non-fiction and administrative overview surrounding business basics.

Position Identified   3

Vast quantities of time are lost inside an enterprise whenever a vacancy is apparent and the extremes that are necessary to prove the 'gap' is endless. Filling the spot with speed is a no-go area as most Human Resource departments are overwhelmed and creative solutions is not included in the mandate.

Recruitment Process Energized   4

Business operations are conducted like the tortoise in the race against the hare – slow and steady progress maintained! Cross checking skillsets with the budget and expense monster sharpening the quill, it is no wonder it takes months to locate a warm body for the post. Inside this arrangement there are ways and means to expedite and communicate internally that solve many issues and engender support for the company and reduce the frustrations for the incumbent staff.

Expense control limits the public announcements heralding that the business needs a replacement. Caution surfaces when this method is encased in practice.

An incredible statistic emerges from the marketplace relevant to assistance within this section. HR professionals should be allowed to utilize their confidentiality and integrity when details requested by a prospective future employer. This may initiate a ground movement in people actually doing the job that they are paid for, without recourse to complaining about the injustices.

It is amazing how fast a person can become by looking solely for incorrect aspects inside a document. The more experienced do not waste energy and are incredibly accurate in their assessment of sloppy material being presented for a role in the company. The OUT basket soon becomes filled as they navigate through the resumes. In these circumstances lessons are there to be learned by individuals who do not take precision and integrity into consideration when sending formal applications to firms.

Organizational skills by the HR Pro is an essential part of the recruitment drive as they strive to bring all concerned to one meeting location. This is no mean feat as they are also required to manufacture an interview process that reveals in depth answers to the questions posed by the selected panel.

The moment of truth arises, and each side of the table is anxious and needing composure, and an opportunity to portray themselves in a positive light. Interviewers taking the time to defuse the apprehension will lead to a much more significant meeting arranged to decide on the expertise identified inside the curriculum vitae.

When determining who the correct hire for the operation is, companies need to be careful on the structure and insight gained from the interaction. Personal bias can limit the opportunities and may create a situation where the 'right' person is overlooked.

Preparation for amassing the intimate minutiae for delivery to the 'chosen one' is vital and becomes another stage of the procedure in landing the employee of choice. Significant dialogue can be expected, especially when a senior member of staff is being replaced – future behaviors or tendencies can be recognized during this phase – 'buyer beware'.

If ever communication is required to introduce and extol the virtues and strengths internally of a new hire, now is the period.

Integration essentials manifest themselves whenever the appointee attends and is under instruction. Building relationships are crucial and must never be underrated. Attention to detail and the personality of the trainers require thoughtfulness as the initial ambassadors for the corporation.

The most enlightening observation points take place during the trial of the individual. Paying close attention to practices and attitudes can be beneficial today and tomorrow for the employer.

The world as we know it is changing and with a gig economy, this title may one day be obsolete.

Attaching a positive or negative declaration to a person's outlook provides an insight into the future tenure. Leaders can be spotted early on inside operations and many companies fail to distinguish the differential apparent in the workspace.

Results are based on real time activities and sales. Each member of the group has a responsibility to elevate and maintain standards complimentary to producing best business practices.

The time to incorporate change is NOW! Involve and create consensus for the actions with each living creature inside the organization.

Essential information is needed when conversing with a person that you have selected to assume a role within the firm. However, contingency plans are required to cover the last minute hitch that can happen. As the motto for the Boy Scouts reads 'Be Prepared'.

Involvement means considering and reaching out to personnel and 'listening'. This action can be difficult to for some managers to endure, but the failure to understand the assets concerns can rein havoc on the parade.

Simplicity is rewarded and when endorsed and supported from

within it can produce outstanding returns for the company and individual.

Each thought and action when collected internally and promoted to a value state sends volumes of positive messages that encourage operating at a higher standard and learning to discuss and share meaningfully, without reluctance to include personal observations that maybe contrary to popular belief.

Varied compensation arrangements are in place all over the corporate world and certain influences reflect the agreements.

Questions are asked in situations if the business was directed by the workers and not the Bosses? What savings and advantages could be gained and would they be sustainable?

There are many ways to demonstrate appreciation for the workforce and the use of rewards is one that can be enjoyed and entertained without 'breaking the bank'.

The demand for creative and productive solutions is never far from the lips of management to satisfy the customer and retain orders arriving with an increased velocity.

Finding leadership and not being afraid to speak one's mind are difficult attributes being sought by many of industry's top companies. Several examples are highlighted colorfully with a fabulous quote used extensively by a successful 'billionaire'.

Lessons to be learned are essential when operating a venture that is tied to maintaining a high level of consistency. Great strides occur when we all row in the same direction!

When the elephant in the room is not identified and clearly removed; 'Houston, we have a problem! Telling an employee some home truths can be very distasteful and many supervisory members baulk at the idea, preferring to turn a 'blind eye' to the situation.

Courageous and integrated discussions within an organization are advantageous especially when promotions are concerned.

Open and transparent business news released to the personnel, especially when associated with profitability and compensatory adjustments increases morale and loyalty.

Adopting a system to record and highlight operational ebbs and flows without attaching blame and fearful consequences takes skill and awareness.

Pressures of work and life can influence and send certain people over the edge. Having methodology in place to support and create an environment based on caring for each other, goes a long way in being a successful employer.

Historically, the 'robber barons' of the 19th century reduced wages and increased hours of work and the well-being of their employees were not high on their agenda. Today, with our society's emphasis on work, life, and balance we can act responsibly and in so doing; enjoy the healthy reputation that it conveys.

successes. Top to Bottom participation in Best Practices reaps results across the organization.

Positive energy flows when a united workforce is all singing the same tune! The strength of an enterprise is felt throughout the business with complementary praise inspiring more involvement.

Acknowledgments

Inspiration and support for the composition of this book come from my friend; Stacey Groom, to whom I am eternally grateful, in the supply of never ending business insight and design for a better world for all of us to exist and cohabit with harmony and decency extended to each other.

Introduction

'If it weren't for the last minute, nothing would get done'

This outlined statement by someone unknown, paints a picture of chaos and uncertainty relevant to the business world. It certainly does not need to be this way as many enterprises spend vast quantities of time deliberating on what to do next!

The quality of the discussions and direction can in certain cases lead to satisfactory conclusions. In reaching this stage there are traditionally many hurdles to overcome and what better way to drive the bus than by inserting a guide or process.

Staff members obeying such orders and instruction willingly follow the route provided and the outcomes generally produce the desired result.

Taking into account what is required to fix a vacancy the machinations of an internal system begins to evolve. Advice, suggestions and skillsets combine to elicit a responsive party willing to assist and join the team. This course of action is performed multiple times within large and small corporations annually. Automated services are available and this can substantially reduce the effort necessary to plug the gap.

In tackling the problem of hiring the best candidate many considerations are required and lording over them are the opportunities to disrupt the present status and incorporate change. Financial data is scrutinized and the tweaking allows adjustment to secure potentially a viable solution, without breaking the bank.

Our employees are the catalyst for pushing the business forward and the manner in which we hunt, locate and ensnare give the advantage to the employer.

Spending time on the cultivation of a new hire creates a bond that when assembled correctly increases the chances of a successful union. Investment in the employee begins prior to the search conducted and the resources working to find the elusive replacement or addition. By taking the steps to open the door and allow creativity to emerge; companies with a desire to advance are easily in the lead by integrating astutely newcomers to their industry.

Workforces across the globe strive to excel and the operations can at times resemble a top secret government run facility. Building into play a collective atmosphere inviting fresh thoughts and inspirations to overcome competitive angles; spreads the pressure of business growth and development across the organization. There are many individuals who will relish the challenge and each case can be measured to exact potential outcomes from the energy and enthusiasm unleashed.

Focusing on the characters already in place adds to their progress and as they feel appreciated; their own personal investment in the company aligns to produce effective consequences.

Support for each member of the team is business intelligence at its finest. Delivering on culture and harmony related programs is oxygen to the labor force and must be sustained through a functioning group of managers. As we operate in the best interests of the consumer and staff certain characteristics will emerge as the mood in the workplace bubbles and downtime decreases.

Feedback becomes important from all areas to establish and maintain positive recognition for operational control and evolution.

Endorsement of Best Practices throughout each phase of the industry lends credence to the reputation being built internally. In a short space of time this will be reflected onto the relationship being forged with the customer and sales targets being exceeded.

As you read this book I sincerely hope that the value of the employee and customer are recognized and can be incorporated into your own business model.

'In all human affairs there are *efforts*, there are *results*, and the strength of the effort is the measure of the result'.
James Lane Allen.

Part 1

HR Due Diligence

Position identified

Large companies recognize that they are short of an employee, through many channels. Constant lateness of filling an order, insufficient break times for on-floor staff, orders not being filled, calls not being taken, complaints on lack of service in the restaurant, food late on delivery and 'cold', premises closed when they should be open, turnover; this list can be expanded and irrespective of why the need is there, action has to be taken to resolve.

No doubt as the reader you are aware of the Human Resource Policy Manuals that abound in many big corporations. The intricate statements addressing the insignificant employee with words, phrases and sentences that appear to come from someone who has swallowed a dictionary and is in the process of reciting it verbatim. However bored you may feel now is not the time to read the version from Company 'Y'. It is suffice to say that many planned hours will be consumed in filling the spot 'urgently', and at a lower price point, especially, if the turnover member was experienced and had shown some form of loyalty and remained within the Corporation for a period of time, earning additional shekel's to the pay packet. Supervisor's bringing forward the news of Imminent vacancy requiring inserting another warm body to the cause, are viewed skeptically as they may be considered as pampering their own nest, and building an empire. Such is the meanness and totally irresponsible view taken by personnel, brought up on saving pennies and losing pounds. At what point you ask is the efficiency meter applied to the Return on Investment of recruiting a person, initiating the training and onboarding satisfactorily, in everyone's benefit. HR do not look at these areas, check the manual and realize the loss factor for the organization is mounting and the process has not yet kicked into gear! The adage Time Management certainly does not apply as 'Vacancy Management' rears its ugly head and cost savings can be incorporated into the scheme without causing too many ripples, as the staff are aware that the HR department is deeply consumed and effectively working on replacement of the employee – LOL! Expense control is paramount to improving the bottom line and even in these types of circumstances; the need to be fiscally prudent is catapulted onto the stage of administration.

Recruitment Process Energized

The manual explains the tried and trusted arrangements necessary to establish the corporate process. From an outsider's point of view there are three speeds being operated: Slow, Dead Slow and Stop. Full steam ahead does not apply as the careful meanderings around setting target dates for meetings to discuss the role of the potential employee with direct reports, adds to the timeline. A review of the previous contract or position description is line-by-line scrutinized with careful additions and deletions included in the final draft that is sent up the line for review and approval. Again, the application of how long this methodology will take is subject to the enthusiasm and inbox of the HR Representative tasked with fulfillment of the opening, bringing in or elevating another crew member to the post. What complicates this situation is whether there are candidates with sufficient skills or abilities in their possession to undertake the role made vacant by the former colleague. This opens the next can of worms in the form of prior Performance Reviews for discussion, dialogue and dismissal of a possible application as they have offended someone in the Executive chair's keen sense of righteousness and could not be considered for such advancement and increased pay scale. Delay becomes the norm for such antics and many corporate HR staff irrespective if they are competent, knuckle under to the pressure of not changing gears and accelerating the route of the staffing method. Bringing forward that the tedious journey could be overhauled and improved is the 'kiss of death' inside many organizations. Learning to follow direction is critical and the adherence to this principle retains many professional and incompetent HR Representatives. In a famous poem by Tennyson –

'Someone had blundered.
Theirs not to make reply.
Theirs not to reason why.
Theirs but to do and die.
Into the valley of death rode the six hundred'…

This is quite dramatic and although many corporate Personnel officers would claim that the recruitment plan does not necessarily bring death to people, it does leave a bitter taste that another more inventive way to recruit is available and all it requires is for 'someone' to stand up and initiate a change. How revolutionary and stream-lined that would propel the world of enlistment! Many organizations do not seek the assistance of current staff to meet the opening with a friend/family member before initiating the task; why, is never explained as the incumbents are aware of the culture and job requirements: pros and cons. Nepotism is whispered, although not too loud!

Advertising

Costs come quickly into the frame as the team looks to open dialogue and exposure in a bigger market. Size of publicity for the role increases costs and in recent years I have noticed how small the positions open within newsprint are becoming. Online notification and Social Media settings appear to be the favorite tools to research and find suitable candidates. All come with a cost, which evidently must be less than the quarter page prior ads – especially if the post is one of an Executive or Senior Management status. Information commensurate with the title is bureaucratese at its best and when reading between the lines, you can see whether someone has been targeted or an Agency has identified someone on their Executive Search lists.

Details surrounding the salary are excluded and generally will involve a comparison range to attract and generate interest for persons seeking a change. Lower level spots do not need or are declared + minimum amounts; not the most productive or creative elements in persuading new blood into a company. It may be effective short-term for the warm body occupying and being a plug-in, be warned about this practice.

Submission of Resume

A search of Google for resume writers brings into the space an industry spawning 83.5million entities willing to provide this service to you; for a cost, of course. Therefore, the anxiety enveloping people wanting to upgrade or send their CV should not be as stressful as first imagined. Many schools are including the writing of the historical employment document for their students. Keeping it simple and eye-catching being key to the acceptance and retention for review necessary to continue in the job hunt. Whilst assisting a company apply for government funding to operate a new Canadian employment program, designed to assist with their career hunting, I was astonished at the array of methodologies being used to get in front of the HR professional. The hours spent writing and deleting personal information by the hopeful was astonishing as they tried to perfect the structure and influence a stranger about their unique skillsets. There are many books and articles written on this subject and I feel that the most effective include a description of the actual individual; honestly and with integrity. It can be assumed that there is enhancement of the roles previously played in other workforces, and the HR Pro will determine the nonsense from the facts. This is why the Human Resource professionals need to be able to assist one another with data surrounding hires, without fear of prosecution. Delivery of the 'history' of an applicant is generally accepted online and stored confidentially before being reviewed. I always like to think that human-centric companies will acknowledge the recipient. Although, I am well aware that many do not. Shame on them!

Screening IN/OUT

In observing corporate HR practices following the arrival of resumes and cover letters, deemed to be a standard for consideration of the applicant's capabilities; the emphasis is to shrink the quantity, therefore, screen OUT and Not In. Thus, reducing time factors as they chop and slice the Inbox to a manageable number that can be assessed and interviewed initially by telephone is key! Reviewing the abilities, history and potential for contemplation to assume the qualifications needed to occupy the role is quite the challenge. Competent and experienced HR officers come into their own in these circumstances. They verbally digest the oral descriptions offered by the aspirant and form opinions through what is not being said, opposed to what is being relayed. Most people do not practice good telephone interview techniques and they come unstuck, failing to have answers to the assortment of superlatives recorded on their personal vita.

By **'failing to prepare'** they have left the organization with no alternative but to screen OUT.

Interview Contact and Dates Set

It is no mean feat to internally arrange dates and times set for the interview progression. Juggling of schedules and responsibilities mean those in-between times, the recruitment officer is establishing a list of questions for the select panel to use as the guide for 'finding' the right candidate. It is never left to the selective group to ask their own questions as this would collapse into chaos and possible loss of the perfect fit. Questions are designed to substantiate the capabilities, experience and abilities to undertake the post above all other applicants. Included in the preparation is a methodology to rank the interviewee's. Normally, this is released to the selected judges prior to the event. A suitable location internally is booked and announced to all concerned. Many times this is a flexible arrangement as operational adjustments may be necessary to accommodate the parties involved. Dependent on the number of interviews set, the panel may review and discuss the merits identifying the rankings on the day. If not, soon thereafter makes sense when memories are fresh and current.

Interviewers Assess Candidates

It is anticipated that the locus selected is suitable and comfortable without disruption to any of the parties. Allowing an opportunity for nerves to be settled the opening remarks by the chairperson of the panel are meant to be informative, confidence building and establishing a working relationship to extract the 'real' potential and in-person strengths of the contender. Each individual on the panel must be sufficiently briefed on the requirements essential for bringing into the group an outsider who will demonstrate value and supplement the workforce. Decorum and professionalism must be validated throughout the meeting as both sides are assessing the other. Understanding the timing and question based manner to acquire and solicit answers within the timeframe are substantial in the overall selection points. Many people need time to reflect and deliberate on verbalizing a response, and the chairperson must be cognizant of this scenario unfolding. Control of the proceedings is not easy and each dialogue is different with complacency never allowed to emerge throughout the get-together. I have witnessed many 'ramblings' by interviewee's with chairpersons not intervening and bringing the respondent back on track. This can be game changing, as naturally the digression is fixated upon by board members within debrief. Also, an overabundance of self-confidence can be a critical part of an interview and the person literally eliminates themselves from selection through egotism. The quality of the questions and the presentation to the interviewee need consistency and must be delivered equitably. Seeing an assessment board member mumbling and fumbling with the diction is embarrassing and decidedly bias towards the candidate involved. My suggestion to all writers of the questionnaire is keep it simple, clear and concise in search of answers. Body language is a factor and is noticeable when the 'hot seat occupier' begins squirming, looking too far off places left or right for replies and including the silence killing 'UM' or 'AH'.

Once again, preparation is an important part of the examinee delivering on the promise potential recognized inside the resume.

Best Fit Acknowledged

Considering that each participant of the panel brings their own prejudices into determining the 'right' type of personality for the vacancy. All recorded thoughts, annotations on the Q/A pages can represent support for what ultimately will be a working colleague is invaluable. Too often fear of speaking up and indicating what their interpretation of the dialogue results in the wrong selection. It is imperative that equal and integrity based analysis be included to ensure fairness and transparency in the progression, to identify and reward the applicant for their efforts. Several organizations add into the mix with Personality based questionnaires and aptitude test to scale up or down the adversaries and this is taken into account as the figures are added. Consensus is applied by the panel and the best **'fit'** goes forward to the next stage of hiring.

Job Offer

Assuming that all goes well in the assessment rankings and a clear winner emerges, the overall package is assembled and re-examined to ensure nothing is missing and that it will be sufficient to entice the 'new' hire to sign-on. Basics that include salary, vacation and benefits are the most intriguing with options to negotiate adjustments, in the upper ranks especially. Most professionals love to haggle on the details as they know the company 'wants' them and they have topped the poll. Time can be wasted in this 2-way interaction and care must be taken that the individual is not playing with their current employer to obtain a substantive improvement in compensation. Many people use the job interview circus to set-up the opportunity for advancing their own situation – slightly unethical, but performed throughout the business world. In certain cases the prospect will have his/her lawyer to review the wording to ensure that a parachute clause is present or added to protect future changes of fortune in the event that the opportunity does not pan out as expected. Personal delivery of the offer can be made with conditions and this may speed up and ensure that both parties are legitimate and encouraged to proceed in a timely manner. There may be additional discussion prior to the 'signing-on' in clarifying certain aspects of the contract and this is beneficial in confirming the right candidate. Taking the time to acquaint a 'new hire' with the accountabilities and responsibilities of the role is part of the 'onboarding' and culture present in the organization.

Open, transparent and critical for future business success is broadcast using this type of communication with the individual!

Hire

Following the administrative functions addressed and satisfied; the actual hire is now imminent. The relaying of the news is and must be extensively released to garner support and satisfy the waiting parties. Internal traditions will apply and be extended to meet all nuances across the staff – 'getting the memo is important' for everyone. Highlighting and introducing a new person to the family requires clever particulars that bring anticipation of welcome and change. This is certainly needed if there have been any local employees included in the search and selection program. It would be prudent to make them aware prior to the release.

Contact with external candidates not making the cut can be performed empathetically. Anything less is downright inexcusable and will lessen the reputation of the employer.

Train

Irrespective of the status of the new hire it is mandatory to advise on business culture and create a genuine impression of expectations. Formal training programs, mentorship and development exposure build trust and inclusion of the Trainee in his/her new surroundings. This positive approach will be rewarded as the need to mix and mingle yield better production and first impressions. Each aspects of the business must be included to create a well-rounded and inclusive vision of the future that they are becoming a part of. It is preferable that a history and evolution within the industry is understood and documented, filling in the market-place competition and encounters that will be prevalent going forward. Follow-up by the HR Pro with the 'new-bie' is important and integral to develop a relationship and observe with feedback and comments on the value added benefits that is now a resource to be unlocked and gleaned. Details surrounding the training generally make their way into the personnel file and are good barometers for next stage advancement or stagnation. Companies making this period of investment into an employee can reap many rewards with fresh eye changes that can be easily implemented and complete with appreciation demonstrated.

All teachings include the building of trust to excel in the best interests of the enterprise and individual.

Ronald Reagan stated, **'Trust but verify'**.

Probationary Period

In plain language most people can 'keep it together' for a short period of time, and as a result some companies have employees for life that impact everyone. In my opinion every new hire must be placed on a contract for the first three years. Thereafter, full time equivalent status can be confirmed as sufficient time to observe, assess and establish the personality, attitude and working habits operationally. This may seem unreasonably harsh, however, in the real world the 'floaters' will do just enough to get by and later their impact will have a telling regard on the workforce. Within the three years observations on absences, respect and character manifest themselves sufficiently to form long-lasting opinions leading to a parting of the ways or a FTE award. Having the strength and conviction to operate like this will be rare in many enterprises. There is no fun when someone hired only a short time ago fails to make the grade and you are responsible to begin the 'axing' procedure. Having clear, unequivocal written documentation addressing the probationary period work performance is the start. The company must be protected by ensuring that all steps to train, educate and support the staff member have been implemented and are beyond reproach. Constant updates personally made to the employee, along with written responses and actions MUST be included in the file. Otherwise, lawsuits may follow for failure to apply the basic fundamental arrangements to integrate the individual. Criticism and targeted negative comments will inevitably follow the dismissal of someone who is aggrieved at the outcome.

That is why I am very concerned that we pander to keep people who fail to match up and become an important part of the organization, because we become complacent on the checklists of establishing competence during this timeframe. Heed the warning!

FTE

To become an accepted Full-Time Equivalent is an honor in today's world of employment. According to statistics, the average person will stay with a company between 5 – 7 years, before they must leave and chase their dream. This means the identification of long term talent with the propensity to stay the course through loyalty is precious. Work that is required to be carried out is measured and determined using many tools and resources. Logical numbers of employees consistent with conducting the duties are calculated and they form the basis for the FTE model to take shape within a department or unit. I always remember speaking with a VP of HR who assured me that it was better to operate 'lean' than overstock the floor with personnel. Keep people gainfully engrossed in working activities and they will overlook their watches and be grateful when a supervisor advises 'break time' is upon us. This also ensures the reduction of idle hands especially when customers are concerned. Many operations have reduced the FTE's and included Part-Time Equivalents into the arena. Reducing expenses and salaries being the motivation and of course the requirement to pay benefits is dramatically decreased, all performed for the wrong reasons and impacting the most valuable assets. It does not work short-term it is a long range goal of many corporate businesses to reduce FTE's, and supplement with several PTE's and Casual labor. This is a disgusting Executive and ownership practice.

'Strong people don't put others down…They lift them up'.
Michael P. Watson

Attitude

It is a recognized fact that more companies are 'hiring for attitude' and training for position. The reasons are simply that you can't train attitude. Individuals either have copious amounts of it, or they have a dismal lack of this component that is invaluable in today's workplace. The kind of attitude I am referring to is one where they want to indulge themselves in the companies industry and are willing to demonstrate their buy-in without having to ask permission to perform at the highest standard. Having this important personal characteristic demands recognition from the moment that contact with the prospect occurs and is continued onto the 'shop floor' with positivity over the incoming negativity that life and disheartened colleagues can lay on the new start. By overcoming the adversity and displaying an ability to influence co-workers is a unique trait that translates to effect occupants of similar roles without the drive. These are leadership qualities evolving and by endorsing and supporting this type of engagement, irrespective of length of tenure, more will be achieved with less. It is noticeable that employees accepting challenges of working under pressure rise above the average with the behavior triggering enjoyment and raising the bar on mentoring others to excel. This strength of character builds a following of fellow employees as they see and recognize a decision-maker among them, paving the way to have others emulate the approach. The lesson learned is to incorporate a Q/A interview process that 'pinpoints' the attitude and tracks the progress.

Performance

Business results are important to everyone connected with the organization and the outcome between each quarter to another must be realized at every level for the benefits affect each person. There must be a collective effort identified and reinforced seeking distinct teamwork participation to achieve the common goal and be deliverable.

Including measurement at each phase of the operation is a necessary evil as it will establish whether the feat is achievable or 'pie in the sky' board room rhetoric for the shareholders axiom. Outlining the target accessibility and inspiring a journey to believe in the plan and to execute wholeheartedly by all involved, brings rewards comprised of financial, confidence and business status escalating globally. Inserting an appreciation and progressive opportunity across the 'work community' allows each employee to get on the wave board and surf the success that this type of activity brings with it. Therefore, communication on progress is vital and not just for the eyes of the management team – include the workforce and build on growth.

Change

Sometimes it takes an operational architect to assess and draw up the lines and avenues leading to internal work change. One simple question always emerges, is it necessary or is there another way? Detailing the method that will take the firm headlong into an area that includes cost factors, personal –v– company adjustments and the anticipated benefits believed to be sustainable, but are they sufficiently attractive to the workforce to endorse immediately or will they be another executive whim treated as an indulgent disposable waste of energy and time. Whatever route being introduced it is mandatory to include a collaborative and involvement participation that creates clear pathways inside the rollout, training and timeline for the change to matter. Every time we initiate change in an organization, management anticipates a profitable outcome that is commented upon in a formal and sometimes informal manner. Measuring the transformation in an upbeat way assists with the uncomfortable way we humans act with change. The way ahead has bonus factors collectively outlined and the inclusive adjustments when incorporated to reflect all our misgivings can be positively stated. Change is NOT a punishment and when we explain change, introduce change, and determine the reasons for change in our workforce we quickly come to appreciate their insight and inclination to change.

Part 2

What Happens?

Opportunity Accepted/Declined/Resisted

One of the key ingredients inside a job offer is to make it easy to accept. This encompasses a suitable and convenient timeline to start with the appropriate compensatory figures included. Documentation for the approval process should contain information on the company's onboarding schedule, culture and welcoming remarks to a dynamic group. In the background, identification of the mentor communicated reliably with the necessary space, equipment and manual for orientation arranged. Clarity of the purpose in hiring this person must be clearly addressed along with the welcome package. We only get the chance to demonstrate our professionalism once! In situations where the job offer is declined take the time to confirm reasons for turning down the position. This will be a delicate 2-way professional response to understand and later explain to the executive and management on the failure to enlist the subject. This does create an opportunity to review without recrimination the proposition and learn from the upshot. Taking the chance to re-engineer the initial offer to #2 on the wanted list from the original hiring panel gives an opening to re-assess the candidate again and determine if anything is missing or odd in the selection and ranking. One of the considerations is in determining the effects on the operation by inserting this 2nd placed applicant? If nothing unveils itself and the instruction to proceed is green lighted, continue and cross fingers for acceptance. There may be times when an offer is made and resisted by the selected party. This can be common in higher-paid positions as people are aware of the Executive search and costs to conduct. In this scenario listen attentively to the material divulged for the resistance and the insight that it will afford the HR officer in adjusting plans. There may be enough content to restart the program and seek new creative solutions to overcome the misconception or status of the position. In the best interests of the company it is advisable to communicate the delay and avoid gossip/rumor developing. During this interval the department can re-consider the facts of the case and act accordingly. This may include changing direction and re-organizing the department and shifting responsibilities. The positive momentum sustained in a search is carried out with the business flow continuing. Alternatives arise from situations and some are unexpected and beneficial to the enterprise, keep a trained eye open for fate playing its hand and accept the compromise.

Engage Employees

De-stress the workplace using clear direction and consistent messaging; take time to listen and collaborate. Avoid discrepancies in combination and Be Fair, Genuine and Involved. Recognize the small things troubling staff as they are in reality 'large things' drawing attention to the front-line and needing corrective action. Swiftly reveal actions to participate and support by involving the entire workforce. Incorporate '*FUNdamentals*' with time to celebrate company and personal achievements. Of course, it sounds 'hicky', but when we accept that **EVERYONE is EQUAL and DIFFERENT** the future becomes more encouraging as solutions emanating from the battle zone carry a significant weight of comprehension. When we creatively organize rewards with the same bonus to ALL – no disparity exists and equality becomes acceptable and inspirational. A recent Christmas bonus paid to 198 employees of a Commercial Real Estate business from Maryland attracted global attention for the $50,000 gift to each member of the staff at the function. Unexpected and worth significant more in loyalty, advertisement and life-changing moments paves the way forward for this group of happy employees. An organization sharing operational numbers during monthly events gives an opportunity for staff to verbalize input and to understand the SOAR of the company. Positive affirmation of the 'We' factor in the operations ensures that the Be Different message is conveyed and accepted within every layer of the enterprise. Management believing in Team approach and knowledge, starts with knowing every member of the Units name and using them when talking daily to the crew. As we appreciate the Wins, so we review the Losses and determining ways to advance involving a Think Tank to Progress. Bill Bellichick, New England Patriots Head Coach is credited with stating *never get too high with a win and never too low with a loss* – remain positive and consistent! It certainly has assisted him and the team to multiple Superbowl wins and a career and legacy that may never be equaled. Business flows need a multi-channel flow of communication – up, down and across. This is similar to the Henri Fayol ladder of leadership – each step represents access to talk and discuss ideas across the organization and up or down with communiqués exploring initiatives and best practices. Launching a business with the right culture is important with an ability to monitor and maintain consistent attention to the spirit and nuances of the philosophy. By instilling these values and commitment to community improvements, employees can recognize the leadership qualities of the business when benefits affect them directly. Childcare, operational flexibility and supportive health care programs with wage and salaries providing living incomes and future investment covered.

These accomplishments highlight a progressive operator and form a clear road to success encouraging open dialogue and action by each member of the personnel.

Common-Sense Platform Applied to ALL Employees

D2SM designed and generated an online program that allows each member of staff to ask questions in the workplace without fear of being ridiculed and regarded as being dumb. Answers deliver to the user a simple, efficient and comprehensive response annotated without being disparaging or condescending. Instilling the details in each employee as they are motivated to use the service and incorporate the material on a daily basis with the most important resource for the business – the *Boss* (customer). This becomes a *Win-Win* as recognition of usage is easily determined by the owner/management with indicators of future supervisory capacity potential. Observing the time spent learning on Customer and Operational Experience benefits the bottom-line and jump starts a culture understanding that becomes a reality with applied work ethics, contact and passion to improve and become customer-centric. The interaction is essential to developing a rapport and surge in relationship establishment. Repeat business and increased sales become the norm when application of the *Common-Sense Platform* is used by everyone in the organization. Maintaining simplicity throughout the insight demonstrated by the platform is instrumental in creating a learning environment without fear of failure or negativity. All the solutions offered are credible, reliable and easy to digest and utilize in their next meeting with a customer or colleague.

Collaboration

Involvement of ALL is the goal in turning the fortunes of a company from zero to profitability and it is achieved by deliberate cohesive practices starting with the culture. Conversation on every step of the way is important and this was recognized when I spent time with Exxon. Their thoughtful meeting times with persons from every department at morning coffee, lunchtime and afternoon breaks – subsidized by the company. Allowing cross-discussion of projects, execution and efficiencies along with the natural flow of human behavior seemed to match perfectly their internal architecture of involving everyone in the process, deliverables and consistent high-end quality of work output. Harmony appears when we are seen as an integral part of the industrial outcomes and our thoughts and actions matter. Increased involvement becomes welcomed and tag in an appreciative society of peers as the solution is accomplished and repeated with each new challenge. Research finds that as Homo sapiens we need the tribe arrangement to generate our acceptance and strength of one another's capabilities. Reliance on each other is a comfort zone of protection and Ice-Age man relied on securing the settlement whilst one slept or went hunting. Connecting to each other without fear of disownment or ridicule is a positive trust factor when incorporated early in the cultural philosophy of the organization. Having the courage, voice and conviction to speak up when initial stages of a project are underway; may be the key to saving massive amounts of budget expenses. It is interesting that certain individuals can see and be critical of the first phase discussion of a project; all stated to hinder the progress and without a solution based endorsement. Overcoming this defense is necessary to proceed with commitment, without eliminating the input from the naysayers.

Taking a 360 degree observation of the puzzle gives us a deeper understanding of the assignments and the hurdles to be overcome collectively.

Contract

Companies negotiate with higher end members of staff agreements that specifically become laced with benefits and are purely performance driven. If the business is floundering then they may find themselves on the 'out'. Enterprises that are thriving trigger extension clause and increased salary and privileges not reserved for the masses. By extension the individual is continuously aware of the need to improve and stay focused on the job in hand. Lesser positions do not experience this type of 'pressure' as they attend for work, conduct scheduled activity and whether their own personal drive is switched on or not – they remain as employees without many of the perks. Performance evaluation reviews consist of did you do your job sufficiently well to merit an increase or enhancement of the pay and benefits. Most employees are not wired like the executive branch members, and therefore, do not have to devote large amounts of time on exceeding market share and upgrading the sales to higher echelons or breaking new ground on plants/factories. So satisfaction and contentment inserts itself with lack of ambition and roots take place in an environment controlled by supervisory direction, and little opportunity to advance. However, by installation of a contract performance based employment system we may see a different work atmosphere. Inside of which is the hunger to perform our work assignments in a manner that is efficient and consistent. The annual evaluation results identify the effort and position retention for another year. Compensatory changes will be subject to minimum recommendations from HR, keeping the pay differentials intact between the operational members.

Collective Agreements may influence the compensatory figures with mild adjustments to benefits for a set period of time with yearly increases being publicized as a win for the working class.

Employee Driven

It is very unusual to find out about a company that is actually being propelled forward by the staff. Generally, the autocratic approach is well ingrained, and the instructional mannerisms by management to achieve the tasks undertaken by the paid hourly staff remains in place. Allow yourself the discretion to indulge and imagine a commercial operation conveyed positively by the hirelings. What elements would occur in promoting and carrying out business in this manner? Would a decrease be realized in turnover, and would the staff members display signs of loyalty and harmony in the workplace? Can any enterprise actually exist using this fulcrum of paid staff and executive, each exerting weight and balance being fought out on a daily basis? Making decisions in the business world are legendary and for some the Captain of the boat is the leader and must have the final decision on which port to dock the ship. The crew all have duties to attend to in sustaining progress and maintaining the vessel. In this regard our picture of an operational organized and proficient workforce is wishful thinking. Trust components would be a major tripping feature and yet by openly discussing and integrating plans and aspirations, many establishments could score an advantage in taking this philosophy to fruition. A previous Executive that I worked for – always spoke in meetings about the balance. He displayed his 'wings', by opening up his arms and cajoled us the operations team to absorb his statement and right the plane by flying with all the weight evenly distributed, constant speed adhered to, and communication relayed to all onboard. Discipline was controlled by each member of the squad and this kept everyone genuine and honest! Industry could do with a dose of reality that involving all the resources fashions a better environment to exist inside. Power is measureable and the way we utilize it determines the respect and support for participation in future projects irrespective of a complete understanding of the direction.

Re-Engagement

Whatever influences the masses and energizes a turnaround of actions, belief and connection is desirable for the business. Sometimes, a process is initiated that becomes counter-productive and time will decide when management severs the course. Open dialogue explaining the reasoning for the change, will cause a cluster of employees to acknowledge the adjustment and be appreciative in returning to normal business rituals. An outcome to the re-engagement found and represented in the bottom-line improvements reveals a perfect opportunity to disclose and approve the performance level. Dependent on enterprise financial restrictions, a luncheon/reward/cake day treat to personally extend grateful praise for this about turn in fortunes, will garner a restored connection inside the group.

Commit to genuine excitement for recognizing the alteration and look to reduce impending proposals that upset the apple cart for the operation.

Time Sensitive

Every aspect of a commercial setup carries with it a clock that is running extremely fast and lack of control is a viable concern. From answering the phone to taking an order whether by voice or by email the clock is ticking and profitability is under pressure. Departments responsible for identifying zones that are inconsistent and time-consuming must factor in human, electronic and logistical overheads. In order to achieve control and attention to detail, demands consistent observation by each party of the little things as they can consume the most of our valuable time. How often do you hear that we are all too busy in our private lives and now with the progression of Internet access and online ordering – we are compelled to work at a frenetic pace in satisfying the demands of the consumer? Being time-sensitive across the operation becomes a cultural drive and must be instilled from day 1 of an employee's life-cycle inside the organization. Failure to distinguish a breakdown on this subject can ultimately lead to a massive collapse. Customers are fickle and if you cannot provide an item within a specified timeframe, then someone else online can! Taking care of customers is a well-known phrase and the speed of your contact whether online or inside the bricks and mortar is an incredibly prized part in delivering Customer Experience. Departmental meetings must never become boring or lack the credibility of sharing intense functioning matters within a timely period. Constructive, brief and concise assemblies are essential and should never be anything other than productive connection points. Alternatives to current practices must be encouraged from the staff insight to explore and engage improved methods to activate judiciously.

Jeff Bezos, Amazon guru and richest man on the planet, always has an extra seat *'open and available'* for the customer at his boardroom meetings – **the '*customer*' is king!**

Inspirational Action

Sparking the enthusiasm collectively remains a mystery that many entrepreneurs and corporate giants wish they could just *'switch on'*. Sadly, life and business flow does not endear us to behave or respond as simply pushing the mechanism that will transform our atmosphere and output, taking same to new heights. We need to find other ways to magnetize the feelings and begin the start of a beautiful excursion into functioning openly without resistance. Therefore, inhabitants of the workforce are alive to finding a guide prepared to demonstrate and proceed without care for the consequences, as it is the right thing to do. Too often we are mortified at taking a chance inside a job, when the answer is crystal clear and constantly stated by the $50 Billion Dollar Man – Dan Pena *'Just F%^*&%g Do It*!. In accepting a no accomplishment mode of operation we are diluting our own capabilities. *Rise up! Rise up!* Having the inclination to begin the change evolves from the courage of our existence and not being afraid to illuminate your colleagues with an attack minded statement! This is similar to the Great War when soldiers were led by their supervisors to go over the top from their trenches with a whistle and the *'up and at'em'* mentality of our forefathers. Many lives lost in review of this practice have refined our approach to this type of military exploit. Inside many office cubicles, retail stores or assembly plant locations, men and women pray for the opportunity and ability to lead the revolution and engender activity that is brave, resilient and combining a crusade with execution that is beneficial to the organization. It is regarded that everyone has that inner resolution to outline a practice bringing empowerment to the *'silent partners'* of introverted staff members.

A champion is generally born whenever the realization that we all can contribute to stimulate our environment without fear of reproach. The **time to act** is when it is seen as essential and in the best interests of all personnel. ***Now!***

Performance Improvement

Relative to employees entering a business and suffering a dismal probationary and training period. Lessons learned for the employer include ensuring that a standard for work operations is in place. Reasons for bringing this awareness forward early in the career of a new hire is that when things go south quickly, responses need to be available and quicksilver in their delivery and display. The application of best efforts matches the adage that following and emulating the leader will result in great workers. In combination with a Best Practices model demonstrated throughout the enterprise and encouraged religiously by everyone on the payroll guarantees success across the board. When all parties are participating; growth, inventiveness and target meeting associate themselves with benefits that bring joy to the company's bottom line, shareholders, management and staff alike. Introducing and applying the right processes takes time, however as Lee Kuan

Yew, Singapore First Minister stated, *'by monitoring, measuring and modifying work activities we can categorize Performance Improvement for the advantages of all'*. In keeping accurate records and conducting analysis on the work-flow we can use the information learned and highlight the attainment of meeting/superseding our targets. As we publicly appreciate the operators responsible the growing consensus is how fortunate *'we'* all are in being involved with a company that recognizes our efforts and applauds them. Extending this visibility across the empire administrators can include bases of collaboration to generate leads in achieving more. Using the well-worn cliché **TEAM** – *Together Everyone Achieves More* can evolve into new territories surrounding upholding the Performance Improvement. By expanding the process and challenging the workforce; status quo can be a thing of the past. Inclusion in the Annual Report and gratitude allied to worker contribution elevates the platitudes over the year with anticipatory results continuing. Drafting positive Standard Operating Procedures and implementing them in conjunction with the joint information received from front-line and management alike satisfies the common ground model. The value of sharing data and insight becomes very noticeable and obvious. Doubters will find it difficult to stay inaudible. In time they may succumb and assist with the evolution of the workplace. Too often Performance Improvements only become clear when final stages of Progressive Discipline are landed on the unsuspecting employee. Collective Agreements and Human Resources directions have indicated various steps to explain the process ultimately leading to dismissal if not complied with. What would be better than a positive reinforcement of changes needed to satisfy the *'standards'* being pursued. By turning the negativity into a venture ably supported, recorded and measured with openness, it is more likely that constructive outcomes will emerge from the strategy. Overcoming obstacles is recognized when fresh dealers are added onto the casino floor and the Pit Bosses calculate that they are slow and not meeting standards. Developing rapport with the dealers and identifying the basic card security, handling procedures, accuracy and control soon brings the speed to the expected number of hands dealt per minute with management gaining an apostle for Best Practices, reliance and loyalty. Persevering with employees not making the cut can pay dividends as you involve them in a newcomer's overview. Use of technology has an impact on the Performance Improvement whether sustainable and this relies on the person responsible for monitoring progress and their unbiased comments. Taking the emotion out of comparisons and making decisions to re-assess the change required to determine if the firm has a strong grasp on reality is a difficult state to be caught in.

Honesty, integrity, and corrective actions can emerge and be an influence on all around us when **'*we*' don't give up on an employee.** Try it!

Reversal of Change of Attitude

How often in the workplace do we hear that someone has fallen off the rails? It is likely that we have determined the data from monitoring results and they have decreased over a period and '*nothing*' has been effective in correction methods. Normally, the immediate supervisor will make comment to the individual in a sly, cunning way followed by reference to the management not being happy with current outputs. Although not the most trusted route to improve or redress an attitude change, it starts at the beginning and then explodes into a paper history report. The time wasted on this ancient man-management system is excruciating and not worth the effort. The moment a problem is identified '*deal with it*' without extremes of critical recording and meetings. Responses will be swifter and each party can relax and focus on generating the proper results needed from the individual as it may be confusion relative to the position or training matters. Irrespective, people are human and mistakes are common in the workplace environment, but they can be corrected and the faster the better for the morale and future employee advancement and allegiance. Supervisors recognizing issues must have the courage to act responsibly and on-time. Failure to do so interrupts an arrangement between the staff member and the firm pertaining to achieving success for the compensation package negotiated. Misery loves company and if we provide a platform from where to release our venom especially when the impact is personal and avoidable, then the enterprise is the overall loser. Educating front-line managers to recognize the signs of operational distress is a massive factor in preparing them for advanced roles in the business.

Fail to Prepare, Prepare to Fail.

Business Advancement

Addressing the spectrum of needs, challenges and placement inside an industry can be enthralling and pressurized towards a suffocating level. Garnering support from all facets of the trade and inviting communications to propel expansion demonstrates a willingness to take sales activities into perspective and attach a reality check on operational progress and opportunity. We are at our best when a clear pathway is understood and the wheels of motion are turning and thriving collectively. Integrating all members of the team into a high-functioning unit strategically zeroing in towards the target acknowledged; reaps benefits attributable to harmony in the workplace with positive outcomes. Contained inside this elixir are the bonuses of upgrading personnel truly deserving promotions and installation in posts suited to their capabilities and emotional concord. Knock on effects occur when obvious actions take place and the right person has been selected to coordinate future activities. Staff is very conscious of the square peg being elected and inserted into the round hole, ultimately causing them to endure into tolerating the lesser candidate through a flawed system.

Progressive Results

What is amazing and energetic to everyone inside the company is when the outcomes are released and the positivity of the numbers are reflective on the work output and drive of each member of staff. This combination is inspirational for the foreseeable future and management can learn more by listening intently to the workforce as we are more likely to divulge inside knowledge when excited and buoyant. Each chance we get to fly the flag and voice our accomplishments about the service and industry is too good to miss! Making your own people proud of their presence and impact creates a family unification and the willingness to continue at the pace originally set in achieving victory against the face of adversity. Once the details have been publicly shared there comes moments to assess and determine forthcoming compensatory arrangements that will satisfy and invest in personnel evolution. Spending time calculating the risk and rewards for the betterment of the organization and staff is instrumental in maintaining solidarity and loyalty within the business. Reaching out and communicating the intent and information behind the adjustments to salaries with gratefulness demonstrates the involvement of the executive and this unique relationship can rally the troops when things go 'south'.

Monitoring/Measuring

Monitoring and Measuring is priceless when conducted equally and proportionally across the lanes of staffing and operational outputs producing conclusions in determining the strength and effectiveness of the management and staff performance. Drilling down into the numbers and efficiencies reveals an understanding of the commercial flow and the associated costs. By using these figures we can establish forecasting and determining needs for growth from the data studied. This attention to detail supports a progressive approach to operating a business and seeking to ensure its longevity in the marketplace. There are many different vehicles used for this purpose and when applied scrupulously across the enterprise many advantages become apparent. Consistent comparisons between individuals and divisional units' results provide a perspective that may not have been evident when taken solely on single based assessments. The importance factor is each employee is aware and cognizant of the observation circle that is scheduled dependent on SOP's. Supportive practices to excel and exceed bridge the apprehension gap that can appear when failure to quantify is not performed. We all share an inherent desire to be lauded for the paid activity and when performed well – why not!

Contact: Employee to Employee

It takes time to develop a trust and confidante nature in discussing work mannerisms being experienced. Normally people will accept and continue performing without recourse to complaining until the *'bottle of emotion is full and over-flowing'*. At this stage the need to share becomes embroiled with telling all and inserting our own persecuted thoughts and hard done by statements. It may not be noticeable initially, but there comes a time when it is observed and related back to the powers that be. In most cases simple dialogue between workmates are innocent and all about life lessons and experiential acceptance of the occasional *'curve ball'* being thrown our way! However, when criticisms become problematic surrounding an operational issue, action must be initiated immediately to resolve. It may be a simplified fix, but then it may also be a complicated interpersonal relationship that is not conducive or allowed under the policies of the day. The fastest method to recover and *'right'* the ship is necessary and must be conducted intelligently, confidentially and with the support of senior management. We all want to come to work safely and be exposed to safe working environments and return to our loved ones the same way we left. By insisting this practice occurs on the shop floor throughout the facility consistently, we guide the operational limits of acceptable behavior. As we spend almost a third of our life working we build up and enjoy many relationships and friendships that can take us outside of the firm. Encouraging and influencing positive associations in the workplace establishes a culture and philosophy with its own energy and familiarity beneficial to all concerned. Executives displaying this type of camaraderie pass on the opportunity to discuss and outline advancements for the business model, clearly seen by the employees. In situations where top managers fail in the business world to converse and socially debate the industry to identify openings that are prevalent; future chances to succeed become lost and the company misses chances apparent from the outside monitor.

Reflection

Benefits internally recognized; whenever the management and union review the Collective Bargaining Agreement both sides offer different viewpoints. Seen as a perk and important part of job stability against a background of negotiated compensatory reductions to the '*nth*' decimal place, a crossroads is determined. Can it be simply stated that the provider is attempting to maintain the health of the staff? A contrary view from the opposite side may be considered as the company '*nickels and dimes*' the contract financial statements. Giving up on benefits to achieve higher % wage increases to later pay for the same benefits without company assistance appears illogical. However, the extreme is not to have any benefits at all and to meet all medical bills from only 1 pot. One solution to recognize the value of having benefits inside any corporation large or small is to communicate on the ingredients of the aid. Too often it is heard that part-time employees are subject to lesser benefits based on their hourly employment. In a society as rich as ours I am sure that equal compensatory practices can be located and introduced to connect the physical and mental health needs of our personnel. Progressive companies understand that young families experience more service requirements than older generations, and the CBA benefits section can be improved to accommodate all ages in the workforce.

Operational Adjustment

When we consider and focus on the meaning of this title it can cause fear and anxiety to the staff. Why? – Obviously because of the relationship inside the organization and the uncertainty that exists in world markets today. Companies have a tendency to keep things silent and therefore the first thought for employees is '*despair*' when announcements are trickled down or released callously to the front-line on future changes to occur. The impact is magnified in these circumstances and we should be cognizant of the turmoil influencing 'our' people when details begin to emerge, however, softly the roll-out is planned. Lives are affected and already the Executive have analyzed the costs factor and determined the path ahead will lead to greater profit margins at the loss of a few souls – collateral damage as they say! What value is placed on their service and alliance with the organization? Identification of the benefits to be gained by the move and covered in superlatives with how smart the Executive team is in saving the jobs of the many with the sacrifice of a few. These details when published make for horrible reading and the mood of the workforce is not improved when it is circulated that no supervisory/equivalent will join their comrades at the Employment Insurance office line-up. Sugar coating the obvious does not work, however the plans to modify the operations can and should involve all parties taking into consideration lessons learned from the past, and other institutes who undertook this type of drastic alteration. By extending and implementing collaborative and communicative bases a more favorable rollout that includes the measuring and recording of the value change. The harshness of the situation can be pegged back with cooler heads prevailing and a more reasonable approach acquiesced. Also, by incorporating a feedback and comments open sourced pipeline of insight; the organization can breathe and grow with the new wealth of data emerging about the adjustment. In fact, the information can establish changes through 'adjustments to the adjustments' for greater efficiency and effectiveness. Overall this effect can influence the harmony and work affiliations bringing out the best in each side – staff and official side. Close monitoring of the emotions, positive or negative emanating throughout the firm is essential for success. The acceptance and rejection can be closely linked to understanding the problem and having the right fixes inserted to avoid dismissal of the conversion. Putting pen to paper and upgrading the SOP's through a draft document and having it overseen by a working party with time to evaluate will assist with the pace of adjustment.

Determining the proper amount of training and methods employed to achieve this task are valuable resources to absorb and continue using for the business future. Not to be lost in all of this administrative and operational challenge is the position of the customer. We should never relax on the role of the customer and our interaction to guarantee ongoing friendliness.

Tillman Fertitta, Landry's Inc. owner in an interview speaks of:

'No spare customers' – He is right!

Monitoring & Feedback

The necessity to have this course of action implemented throughout the organization makes sense as it gives management the overview of operations raising awareness of outcomes currently being performed. History of the previous financial status against the existing situation allows for a certain amount of deep-thinking to confirm realistically on the foot traffic in a brick and mortars or online operation. Consolidating our thoughts prime us to take the necessary steps over a selected timeline that cannot be allowed to run forever. All responses recorded are valuable viewpoints and together they can influence the Best Practices to be adopted quickly without recourse to delay or indecision. Always looking at the future growth to assess and be aware of impact felt when failing to be decisive for the good of the enterprise. As previously stated measuring and recording value change gives us samples of the effects that output targets and achievements are rated. Including the workers in this process can be advantageous, as all outcomes are reflected on their involvement and alterations in the flow of duties and activities manifest themselves in an array of results. Positive or negative figures are gathered and analyzed from the data surfacing and the contents are the source of congratulations or misery for the bottom-line. Always ensuring the customer has the chance to speak directly with the organization and in a fair and impartial consistent manner assists with understanding the 'flow' of the job inside the business.

One of the Customer Service Commandments is:

'*To make the customer feel important and appreciated*'.

In adopting this approach, you will succeed!

Support Action

In using the acronym POP (Plan, Organize and Prepare) we give our-selves an opportunity to involve every member of the group as we strive to sell the operation. By including the staff the collaborative features can bring out the best of industries hands-on participants and when coupled with a communication policy everyone has a chance to understand the requirements and demands of the commercial undertakings. As the POP continues we begin to recognize various achievements from separate divisions and it stretches us to highlight the attainment. For as we know '*every action has an equal and opposite reaction*', therefore it is central to our scheme to determine the result and applaud the efforts altogether. By opening up this realm of transparent management, staff is cognizant that changes will occur and generally with the release of this information, they will accept the provisions. Making adjustments for the sake of making change is not fruitful or healthy in a unionized environment. However, when acting in the aforesaid manner employees can appreciate the movement necessary to turn the fortunes of a company around and they will be more than willing to assist when requested. At this stage of the procedure the cost benefit effectiveness of the program will be known and should be collectively released. In realizing that the operational balance has been restored and the desired effects of the action confirmed, a sigh of relief is felt and the harmony inside the workplace brings waves of enthusiasm and tensions are observed deescalating. Contained in each step of POP are lessons to be learned and when fed into future operational projects with the emphasis on meeting the Needs Requirement of the individuals matching the goals of the enterprise. Powerful forces are launched in situations bringing every element of a company to life and interactive practices demonstrating that each employee's inclusion matters.

Picasso stated, *'Action is the foundational key to all Success'!*

Harmony & Culture Enhanced

Starting with the first day of employment and continuing throughout their career; expectations clearly identified and directed guarantees each member of staff a safety net to embrace themselves in an environment designed to exceed. In acceptance of the condition employees culminate internal satisfaction, building a collective working grade standard ensuring organizational benefits that are far reaching with a shared responsibility between staff and supervisors. By tightening the mesh around our community, teamwork becomes a fixture with allegiance and trust exploding across the ranks. Company fortunes are one of the first areas to demonstrate the upsurge in perfection with pride felt and described through cooperation and input from both parties: staff side and executive. This greater cohesion occurring within paves the way for in-house investment in learning collectively. By establishing the foundation and indicating the importance of revisiting and maintaining the connection between harmony and culture; reputation is built on this solid base with no substitute allowed.

Many Executive Search and Recruiting firms advocate for companies to adopt certain characteristics when seeking to attract and retain top talent to their business *'Attract the Best and Be the Best'!* Now you know.

Performance Review

Generally described as an annual blood-letting event at some locations with stresses and strains felt throughout the organization as people react to the administrative critique and delivery methods. No one is safe from the Executive to the hourly paid staff, contractors and clients with special emphasis on the AP/AR aspects of the dollar flow involving the contracts negotiated, not always in the favor of the company. We are all susceptible to being scrutinized without anesthesia for the operational numbers and held personally responsible for the 'gap' in meeting the target. The analysis should also incorporate the business flow arrangements and take into consideration all known factors distorting the results. Too many establishments fail to properly establish the connection between services central to the core business and whether value for money is being realized in retention of personnel. This also works in reverse; some staff members do not correlate the lack of quantities as being reflective of their dismal performance. Management bears the brunt of criticism when workers do not grasp their position in the **'great scheme of things'**. Fixes for this puzzle lie in the competition for employment spaces and market share. Each is essential for growth in any industry and the need for vigilance, integrity and functionality to employ and develop staff and products beyond the rivalry of similar businesses. Time is the enemy as we are all busy and having feedback from every side of the operation needs constructive control disseminating fact from fiction. The pressures to yearly report on direct reports, mentors, supervisors and management is an area worth taking the time to evaluate and implement efficiency standards in complying with the HR Policy. There are without doubt significant positives and negatives in the process. Each can be attributed to losing potential high-performers through lack of clarity, realism or honesty. Contribution equally sourced must be present in the final report and be explained simply without malice or fear. An appreciation for service goes a long way when handling one-on-one interviews. Taking the time to divulge and open positively about the association between employee and employer is monumental in creating the 'sandwich' style report. Implementing positive remarks on the outside edges of the sandwich and placing a negative statement in the middle assists with easing the disappointment of being criticized. Many people do not recognize the methodology being used and fixate on the central contents of the sandwich – the critique. **_'Telling it like it is'_** within a Performance Review is not always the most cohesive selection of approaches that can be considered. In looking to avoid the confrontational response it is better to have a series of meetings coordinated to assess a low number of key components of the job. In this way over a period of time a relationship can be entered into that is beneficial for both parties. Waiting a year to present controversial declarations of opinion on an individual is asking for an explosion caused by embarrassment and insult to their personal identity. Avoid this methodology and adopt a more humane and 2-way communicable intercourse that serves the purpose and mandate of the subject. Twelve months in any position allows for experience and reflection to maximize and justify their insight in the role and whether the justification for performance rankings is accurate. Guinness plc. many years ago gave employees an opportunity to self-evaluate. In one instance an office employee over a three year period did not give himself an increase as he considered his personal exploits as not being sufficient for a pay raise. The company afforded him the average salary increase for his honesty. When bonus rewards exist for employees based on the outcomes of the review, a tremendous care and oversight is required to ensure proper administration without conditions attached. Imagine the surprise and excitement felt by a writer of a financial article in a newspaper that inspired Charlie Munger, Berkshire Hathaway Billionaire Vice-Chairman to send him $20,000 for his informative and interesting column. No prior connection or discussion between Munger or the Reporter existed and the *'bonus'* for doing his job was not from his employer. Maintaining high standards and expectations remain the mandate of employers across the land and employees in meeting the challenge must continuously be conscious of the attitude that they display as it will be commented on within the annual showdown of their job accomplishments. My own preference for a Performance Review is to initiate a 3-Part: **START – STOP – CONTINUE** observation on the work being carried out as it has the capabilities of being completed monthly and avoids the distraction at year-end. The #1 organizational objectives for firms is to 'believe in each other' and become Employee – Customer – Company centric.

In this way all roads return to the 3 ring circles made famous by John Adair, Management Theorist who identified the overlapping three rings consisting of ***achieving the task, managing the team or group, and managing the individual.***

Belief

Represented inside many regions are companies that are ranked at the top of their industry with positive energies and vibes being displayed by employees? It is no secret that in order to maintain and safeguard improvements in the workforce, all must participate in the program. This equal approach to support each other is created through the installation of Best Practices across the enterprise group. By instilling the accessible and flexible operational activities brings self-reliance and the realization that problems don't exist as a solution will be found across the workforce. Customers recognize the attention afforded to them and appreciate the relationship as it is initially developed from complimentary interaction inside the firm. Staff happy with their lot demonstrate higher work output figures with efficiency and time effective performances. Company interests are highlighted when work practices are collectively endorsed and routinely acknowledged as the cause for maintaining quality and the competitive edge over the other suppliers. Following the **KISS** (*Keep It Simple Structure*) syndrome and adhering to it jointly emanates confidence in meeting challenges as a group.

Steve Jobs said ***'a lot of companies have chosen to downsize, and maybe that was the right thing for them. We chose a different path. Our belief was that if we kept putting great products in front of customers, they would continue to open their wallets'.***

Optimism

Companies constructed on **SOAR** (Strength, Opportunities, Aspirations and Results) display an enthusiastic higher energy level than other adversaries in the industry. Emotions run deep as everyone is vying for the spot on top and positive affirmation across the facility buoys the mood and increases the application to respond progressively. Anticipation for the future is fuelled when public release of data favorable to the marketplace is assessed. The atmosphere inside the organization exceeds expectations in a supportive and confident manner that influences the creative edge for business development. This is the perfect time to nurture and promote team building and work ethic accomplishments especially using the cooperation between divisions to cement the relationship. Partnerships established with unique personality traits inside and outside the corporation bring strong presence to the sales table. Also, when the workforce is focused on being part of a number one drive campaign, little confrontations and squabbles over minimal items become incidental and easily forgotten. Ideas delivered and generated increase in voracity and the collective attitude is extremely passionate about upcoming ventures. The company stature becomes prominent especially when unrestricted release of outcomes is publicly recognized on the backs of the workforce strengths and skills. It is noticeable during this period that a decrease in absenteeism will be a contributing factor in maintaining the assurance for the longevity of the firm.

'Be fanatically positive and militantly optimistic. If something is not to your liking, change your liking'.

Rick Steves.

Afterword

Initially, when entering the workforce we do not appreciate that behind the scenes a lot of singular and joint activities has taken place. The department heads and human resource specialists all converge to understand what is missing within the company environment and how to achieve quickly the desired result of filling the vacancy.

From the original identification that a new hire is necessary to plug the gap and then into what skill sets are required to amalgamate and be productive ASAP.

Each area of the book expands on my experiences and close observation of the absurd and rational. I make no bones that there will be people who see themselves identified and that is LIFE!

A better living and working society is vital for the improvement of everyone on the planet.

The extremes of poverty and wealth are mixed side-by-side and on each continent! Nowhere is exempt from the realization that people in need are close by and our personal obligation should be to assist without fear and demands for compensation.

This book provides a checklist to assist decision-making and opportunities for persons that are willing to become involved and support the company SOAR!

Notes

A special thank you to the persons whose words and actions have been added to improve the quality of this book:

Sections

Recruitment process recognized
...Alfred Lord Tennyson poem highlights from 'The Charge of the Light Brigade'.

Submission of Resume
...Google search engine.

Train
...quote from Ronald Reagan

FTE
...quote from Michael P. Watson.

Engage employees
...quote from Bill Bellichick, New England Patriots and information stemming from...Henri Fayol 'ladder of leadership'.

Collaboration
...Exxon operational practices.

Inspirational Action
...quote from the $50 Billion Dollar Man, Dan Pena.

Performance Improvement
...quote from Lee Kuan Yew.

Operational Adjustment
...quote from Tillman Fertitta, Landry's, Inc.

Support Action
...quote from Picasso.

Performance Review
...operational activities from Guinness plc,
...personal actions by Charlie Munger, Berkshire Hathaway and
...3 Ring Circle author John Adair, Management Theorist.

Belief
...quote from Steve Jobs, Apple.

Optimism
...quote from Rick Steves.

1% of sales will be donated to the Pledge supporting others less fortunate.